The Everything
Book of
CATS
& KITTENS

Project Editor **Satu Fox**
Author **Andrea Mills**
Designer **Mo Choy**
US Editor **Jane Perlmutter**
US Senior Editor **Shannon Beatty**
Consultant **Bruce Fogle MBE DVM MRCVS**
Pre-Production Producer **Dragana Puvacic**
Senior Producer **Amy Knight**
Jacket Designer **Eleanor Bates**
Jacket Coordinator **Francesca Young**
Creative Technical Support **Sonia Charbonnier**
Managing Editors **Penny Smith, Deborah Lock**
Managing Art Editor **Mabel Chan**
Publisher **Mary Ling**
Art Director **Jane Bull**

First American Edition, 2018
Published in the United States by DK Publishing
345 Hudson Street, New York, New York 10014

A catalog record for this book
is available from the Library of Congress.
ISBN 978-1-4654-7009-6

DK books are available at special discounts when
purchased in bulk for sales promotions, premiums,
fund-raising, oreducational use. For details, contact:
DK Publishing Special Markets, 345 Hudson Street,
New York, New York 10014 SpecialSales@dk.com

Printed in China

A WORLD OF IDEAS:
SEE ALL THERE IS TO KNOW
www.dk.com

Contents

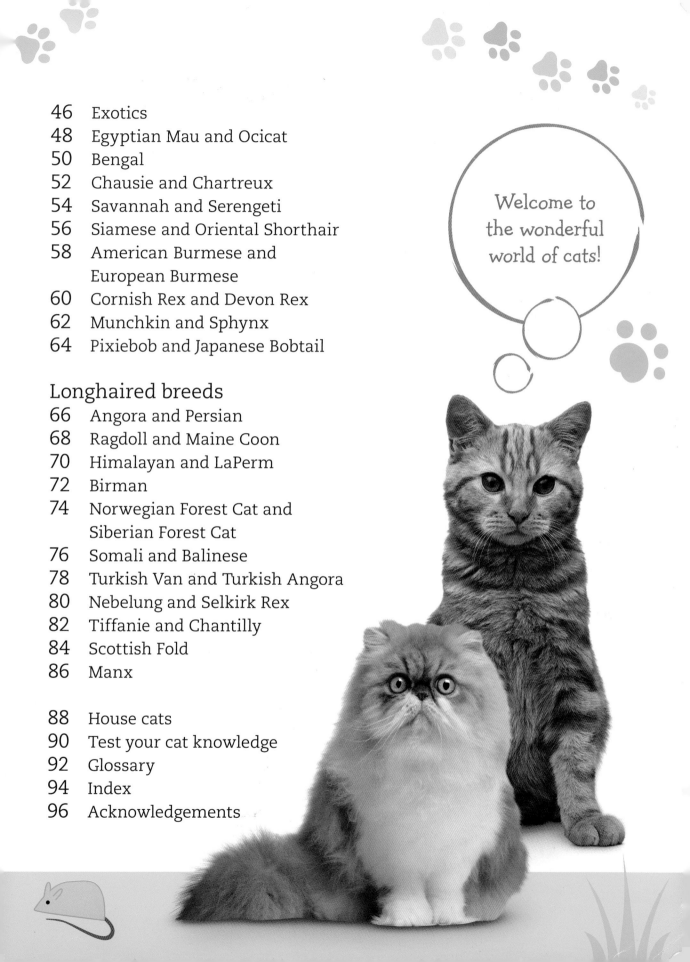

Welcome to the wonderful world of cats!

World of cats

Fantastic felines are the world's most popular furry **pets**. They are found on every continent, except for icy Antarctica.

Maine Coon

The mighty Maine Coon is the oldest cat breed in the US.

Wild cats
Excellent hunting skills help wild cats survive. The largest wild cats are called the big cats. This group includes lions and tigers.

Bobcat

The short-tailed bobcat is the most common wild cat in North America.

North America

Pet cats
In the past, small wild cats were kept to hunt mice. Over time, they became tame. Today, there are many different breeds of pet cat.

There are 100 million pet cats in North America.

South America

The jaguar is America's only big cat.

Jaguar

All pet cats come from **African wild cats**.

European Shorthair

This sweet-natured cat was first bred in Sweden in the 1980s.

Japanese Bobtail

It's easy to spot this breed because it has a supershort tail.

The patterned Eurasian lynx is hard to spot in thick European forests.

Eurasian Lynx

Europe

Asia

Tiger

Australian Mist

This cuddly breed likes to stay indoors.

Cheetah

Africa

The cheetah is the world's fastest land animal.

The tiger is the biggest, heaviest cat in the world.

Australia

Abyssinian

This very old African breed looks a lot like the cats in ancient Egyptian art.

Australia
had no cats until European settlers arrived in the 1700s.

Little and **large**

Cats come in all different sizes. The biggest breed is the enormous Maine Coon, while the tiniest is the small Singapura. Maine Coons can weigh four times more than Singapuras.

67 inches

16 inches

8 inches

The Singapura and Maine Coon next to a woman of average height.

The ears are large compared to the body size.

Singapura

These playful pussycats love being with people. They come from Singapore.

Short, silky fur covers the small, muscular body.

The **Maine Coon** is the **biggest pet** cat.

Maine Coon

These big and beautiful cats from America enjoy eating, playing, and even swimming.

The long, fluffy layers of fur need a lot of brushing.

Strong legs support the body's big bones.

From **top** to **tail**

Cats are designed to be great hunters. Their brilliant balance and super senses help them to climb, jump, run, and pounce. Even pet cats have wild instincts.

Ears have more than 20 muscles.

Nose is very sensitive. It is mostly used for smell and touch, but also to greet other cats with a nose rub.

Whiskers are supersensitive hairs. Cats use them to judge where things are and figure out whether they can squeeze through tight spaces.

Paws release sweat through the chunky foot pads.

A cat **Skeleton** has 230 bones—24 more than yours!

Eyes have pupils three times bigger than people's eyes. They let in more light, so cats can see in low light.

Tail helps balance when jumping, or walking along narrow fences.

Legs are *so* strong that cats can jump 6.5 ft (2 m) straight up.

Cat facts!

Cats have a special organ on the roof of their mouths which lets them smell the air more deeply.

Cats can sleep for up to 18 hours a day. They dream just like humans do.

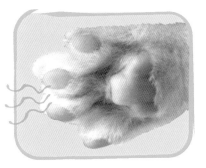

Every cat releases its own chemical scent through its foot pads. This smell is used to mark its territory.

Fantastic furry felines

Cats are a type of mammal, so they are covered in hair. They come in many colors.

Blue
Despite its name, a blue coat is gray with a hint of blue, rather than bright blue.

Calico
Multicolored calicoes have a mix of black, white, and orange fur.

Tabby
Named after a striped cloth from Iraq, tabby cats have striped fur like tiny tigers.

Cat allergies are caused by their saliva, not their fur!

Hair types
Cats usually have three types of hair. They each have a different job to do.

Pointed

A pointed body is a light color with darker parts on the ears, face, paws, and tail.

Orange

Male orange cats have brighter orange fur than female ones.

Black

True black cats have fur coats in one solid color.

White

Cats with white coats have no color at all in their fur.

Guard hairs

The top coat is made up of long guard hairs that keep cats dry.

Awn hairs

A layer of stiff awn hairs protect the cat from bumps and scrapes.

Down hairs

Soft, fine hairs called down keep the cat's body warm.

11

Furry family

Mother cats take care of their kittens by feeding, carrying, and cleaning them. Kittens have lots of brothers and sisters, so growing up together is loads of feline fun!

Each **kitten** has its own **nursing nipple**.

Did you know?
A mother cat can tell its kittens apart just by the way they smell.

Mother's milk
After birth, kittens need their mother's milk. They nurse up to **eight weeks** before they are **weaned** and ready to eat meat.

Keeping warm
with snuggles is good for kittens, whose tiny bodies get cold easily.

Nursing from the mother's nipples is how kittens get their milk supply.

Mother cats carry kittens gently in their mouths to keep them safe.

A litter is usually about four kittens and they are often various colors.

Growing up

Newborn kittens start out as tiny **balls of fur**. But things change fast! Within a year they are **fully grown**, with all the **skills they need**.

A newborn kitten can fit in the palm of your hand.

Eyes are blue in the first weeks of life.

One day old
The kitten's eyes and ears are closed.

One week old
The kitten puts on weight and opens its eyes.

Cat birthdays
A cat grows quickly in the first two years of its life. These years are the same as the first 25 years in a human life! After that, each cat year is equal to four human years.

Kittens cannot **see** or **hear** completely until **three weeks old**.

The fur is thicker and the body is much bigger.

The kitten is curious and eager to explore.

Three weeks old
The kitten stands and takes its first steps.

Six weeks old
The kitten can now run and jump.

Life lessons
Kittens are little copycats. They learn by watching their mothers and then doing the same thing. Playing with the rest of the litter also teaches kittens to react in different ways, from learning to fight to being friendly.

House rules

Taking care of a pet is a big **responsibility** for you. Follow the rules to take care of your cat.

Petting
Give your cat lots of love and affection, but stop when it has had enough!

Cat checklist

Cats need food, love, and fun, just like you do! Pamper your pet by checking off this list of things to remember.

Feeding
Serve dinner at the same time each day so your cat knows the routine.

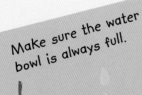

Make sure the water bowl is always full.

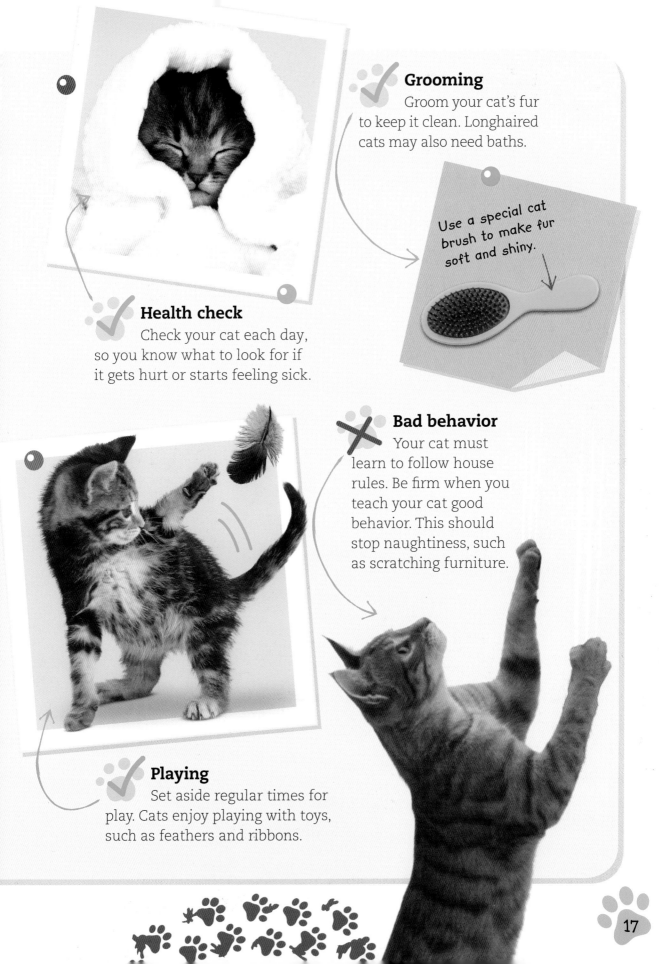

Grooming

Groom your cat's fur to keep it clean. Longhaired cats may also need baths.

Use a special cat brush to make fur soft and shiny.

Health check

Check your cat each day, so you know what to look for if it gets hurt or starts feeling sick.

Bad behavior

Your cat must learn to follow house rules. Be firm when you teach your cat good behavior. This should stop naughtiness, such as scratching furniture.

Playing

Set aside regular times for play. Cats enjoy playing with toys, such as feathers and ribbons.

Paws and claws

Inside furry feline **paws**, you'll find the sharpest, strongest claws! Cats have claws made of keratin, which is the same substance as in our fingernails. Cats' paws have thick, soft **pads** so they can move silently.

*Soft **paws** spread the cat's **weight***

On the move

Cats are marvelous movers. They can crouch down low or leap up to seven times their own height. Their bodies twist and turn easily to hunt or fit through small spaces.

Cats have four toes on their back paws, each with a claw.

Sharp claws can grab prey or grip for climbing

Cats have five clawed toes on their front paws.

Tiptoes
Cats walk on tiptoes, which helps them walk along narrow fences.

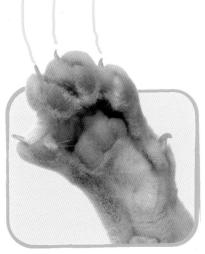

Claws
Cats keep their claws inside their paws when moving around, and bring them out quickly when needed.

Did you know?
Cats climb trees by gripping with their claws. But they get stuck because their claws have no grip when heading the other way!

Cat characters

Think about how different all your friends are. Cats are just the same, with lots of **personality types**.

Forceful
A strong spirit and pushy character help this cat get its own way.

Curious
This playful cat is interested in absolutely everything!

Older cats are

Kitty cats
Kittens share many of the same personality traits while growing up.

Active
Lively kittens love running and chasing in the backyard

Friendly
Social kittens make lots of noise and show their affection.

Friendly
A contented cat, this type likes company and loves cuddling!

Shy
A quiet type, this cat does not like too much time with people.

Spontaneous
This cat likes exploring outdoors, playing games, and welcomes all distractions!

bossier but quieter than young ones.

Adventurous
Kittens find themselves at the center of all kinds of adventures!

Playful
Peekaboo! Hide-and-seek shows a kitten's playful streak.

Independent
When kittens are on the move, they often go exploring.

Sleepy
After constantly being on the go, it is time for a catnap.

ZZZZZ

Body language

Cats can't use words, but they can tell us their feelings with their bodies. Learning their **body language** will help you understand your own little tiger.

Only pet cats walk with their tails upright.

Cats like having their ears petted.

Sign of affection
Cats rub their heads against people to show their love, and also transfer their own smell.

Healthy cats have soft, silky fur.

Knead to know
Cats have a habit of kneading (pressing down) with their front paws. Experts believe this comforts the cat because it reminds it of kneading its mother's tummy to help milk flow.

Telling tails

You can figure out your **cat's moods** by understanding its tail. This does not work for breeds with **no tails** or **short tails**.

Friendly
This cat has its tail held high to show confidence and happiness. Complete catisfaction!

Calm
A low-lying tail means this cat is feeling calm and relaxed, and enjoying its surroundings.

Approach with caution
A scared cat will crouch down low with its tail wrapped underneath its body.

Stay away!
An arched back and tail pointing downward means the cat is angry or scared.

Cats will often turn their backs to their owner while they are on the lookout. This means that they trust you not to attack.

Meowing and talking

Certain people are more talkative than others, and it is the same with cats. Learn their language, so you can understand cat conversations!

This cat wants **food!**

Meow!

Fur baby
In the wild, only kittens meow. Adult pet cats meow at people, because they see us as their parents!

Meow A meow is the most common sound. Cats meow at their owners when they want food or attention.

Kitten sounds
Kittens make more noises than fully grown cats. They learn early on to meow to their mommies when they want something!

Adult sounds
Older cats are generally quieter. However some breeds, such as the Siamese, are much more talkative than others.

Purr

Purr

Purr

Purr When a cat is relaxing or resting, it will often purr to show complete contentment.

Hiss This warning sound means stay away. A hissing cat is scared or angry, and ready to attack.

Yowl This long, moaning sound means your cat is having a bad day!

Hiss!

Yowl!

Chirp A curious cat will make a birdlike chirping sound to show interest in something.

Chirp

Growl This rumbling noise suggests the cat is feeling scared or angry, and should be left alone.

Grrr!

Super senses

While you're fast asleep in bed, a secret world is waking up. From wild cats hunting at night to pet pussycats out for a twilight prowl, felines have senses designed for the dark.

Cats can hear very high-pitched and low-pitched sounds

Night-light A cat's dark pupils get bigger at night to allow more light to enter the eyes.

Bright light The pupils narrow to black slits during the day when there's lots of light.

Whiskers help a cat figure out how close objects are in the dark

Cats can see as well at **night** as in **daytime**.

Eyes open wide so more light can flood into the eyes

Pointed, triangle-shaped ears can move in the direction of any tiny sound.

Cats have a special reflective layer in their eyes that bounces almost all light to the back of the eye.

Whiskers are very sensitive, long hairs. A cat can fit through a space the same width as its whiskers.

Night stalkers

Cat senses are much more developed than ours. This is why they like nighttime when they can see, hear, and smell without being seen.

Hunting habits

Cats have all the strength and skills needed for **hunting**. Unlike wild cats, pet cats are given dinner, but they still like **chasing** birds and mice.

Killer instinct
Even pet cats have a natural instinct to hunt and kill prey.

Mighty muscles
The powerful body is packed with muscles for quick leaps and grabs.

Silent stalker
Cats can sit quietly watching their prey for a long time before pouncing.

Athletic body
The cat's flexible body is designed to run at high speed.

Excellent eyesight

Cats have sharp eyes for any movement, even at night.

Sharp claws

Cats grab their prey by gripping it with their claws.

Plans of attack

On the prowl

A cat hunts by keeping its body low to the ground as it gets ready to pounce.

Gone fishing

Keep an eye on the fish tank! Cats can dip a paw in and try to hook out a fish.

Hunting trophy

Cats may bring home prey to show off their hunting skills or give a gift to their owners!

Feline foodies

A healthy diet is important to keep your feline feeling fine! All cats are **carnivores**, which means they eat meat. This can be given in the form of wet, fresh, or dry food, with plenty of water.

Taste test

Give your cat different flavors of food to see which it enjoys most. Change the menu regularly to keep your cat's interest.

Here, kitty!
Kittens have smaller tummies, so they eat smaller meals, but more often.

Cats have one big main meal a day.

Sugar free
Cats can't taste sweet things, so they have no interest in cake.

Fish Cats may get sick from raw fish, so only give them cooked fish.

Kitty's menu

Wet food

Cats usually enjoy the fabulous flavors of wet food. The wet form is perfect for helping kittens move on from milk and older cats take in water.

Fresh meat

Meat is packed with protein, which gives cats the energy they need. Beef, chicken, and turkey are favorites, but be sure they are cooked properly.

Dry food

Kibble is hard and dry. Biting into it keeps teeth and mouths healthy and clean. Dry food can also be left out all day as a cat snack.

Water

Cats should drink lots of clean water every day. This keeps their bodies healthy and helps them digest food. A cat soon becomes sick without water.

Chocolate Never give your cat any form of chocolate because it can be deadly.

Milk Cats can have milk only as a rare treat since it upsets their tummies.

Cat company

Who wouldn't love having a **friendly fur ball** around? But cats are much more than this for their owners. A cat becomes a **friend**, proven to make people feel happier.

Shared feelings
If you're sad, it can be helpful to talk to a pet about what you're feeling.

Cuddly cat
Although cats are very independent, many enjoy cuddling as much as we do!

Healthy heart
Cats are so relaxing that owners may be less likely to have a heart attack.

Cat therapy

Cats bring such good vibes that they are taken to hospitals, homes for the elderly, and schools for children with disabilities. People love to pet furry felines.

Healing helpers

The soothing vibrations of a cat's purr makes almost everyone feel more relaxed.

Calming cats

Petting cats lowers people's blood pressure.

Cat-friendly home

Bringing a new pet home for the first time is exciting. When the surroundings are safe and comfortable, cats soon settle in with their new family.

Make sure your plants are safe for cats. They can get sick from chewing on the leaves.

Brush and scratch

Brushing keeps fur neat. Cats love to scratch things!

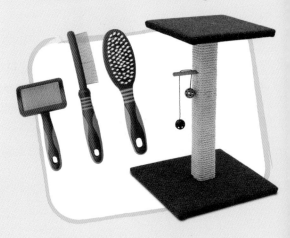

Catnip has a smell and taste that cats love.

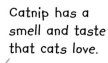

A cat flap lets your pet come and go.

Safe transportation
Cats travel well if trained young and given comfy carriers.

Cat gear

Before your fluffy bundle arrives, prepare your home with all the things a cat needs. Don't forget some delicious treats!

Catnaps A big basket lined with a blanket is ideal for sleeping.

Dinner's ready Always leave out two heavy bowls of food and water.

Let's play Colorful toys and eye-catching objects provide lots of fun.

Toilet time Cats use a litter box for their toilet, which needs to be scooped daily.

True or false?

Stories surround cats. We hear all kinds of things like cats **love** milk, cats **hate** dogs, and cats have **9** lives. So, what is **the truth**? Let's sort out the facts from the fantasy...

TRUE

Cats can be queens

True—A pregnant cat is called a "queen!" A pregnant cat eats more than usual and spends a lot of time in her basket to stay warm and dry.

Cats are ancient pets

True—The bones of a pet cat and its owner were found in a grave on the island of Cyprus. The bones are nearly 10,000 years old!

The ancient Egyptians worshipped cats as gods

True—Cats were considered gods in ancient Egypt. Their goddess Bastet was half cat and half woman.

Egyptian goddess **Bastet** was the protector of cats.

FALSE

A cat has 9 lives
False—This common saying is not true. It is based on the fact that cats can survive short falls by turning in the air to land on their feet.

Cats hate swimming
Mostly true—Generally, cats do not like getting wet. However, wild tigers and the Turkish Van breed do enjoy a dip in the water.

Cats drink milk every day
False—This is a definite no-no! Water is the main drink for cats. Milk can upset their tummies.

Cats hate dogs
False—If cats mix with dogs and other animals starting at an early age, they often get along well together.

There are more than **100 cat breeds**.

American Shorthair

America's oldest cat is bigger but slimmer than its chunky cousin, the British shorthair. This breed arrived with early settlers to America and its main job was mousing. Today this cat is a graceful mover with a friendly nature.

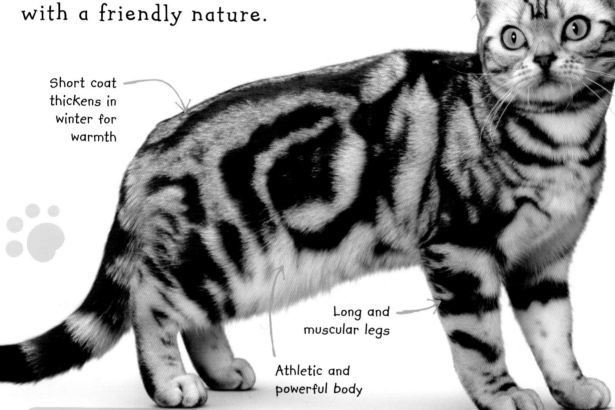

Short coat thickens in winter for warmth

Long and muscular legs

Athletic and powerful body

Fact file

- 🌐 **Origin:** USA
- ↗ **Size:** Medium to large
- ⚖ **Weight:** 6–15 lb (3–7 kg)
- ❀ **Color:** Variety of colors
- 🐾 **Character:** Intelligent, loving, relaxed, and affectionate
- 💬 **Voice:** Quiet

British Shorthair

Britain's most popular pedigree cat is the friendliest fellow around. Often compared to a teddy bear, the shorthair is lovely inside and out. This breed comes in many colors, but the showstopping blue is the most eye-catching.

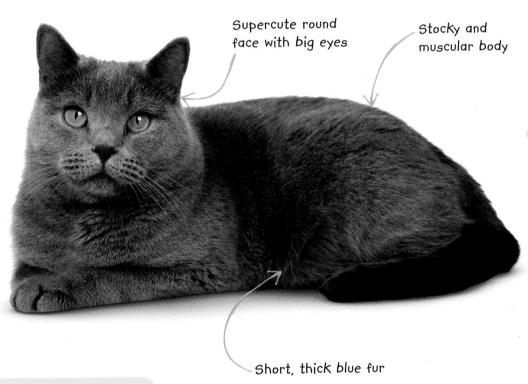

Supercute round face with big eyes

Stocky and muscular body

Short, thick blue fur

Fact file

- **Origin:** Britain
- **Size:** Medium
- **Weight:** 10–18 lb (5–8 kg)
- **Color:** Variety of colors
- **Character:** Kind, loyal, social, and playful
- **Voice:** Loud purr

Australian Mist

This shorthaired cat from Australia is always on the chase in a throwback to its early days hunting mice and other rodents. But once playtime is over, you are guaranteed affection!

Solid and strong body

Shiny **silver** fur

Fact file

- 🌏 **Origin:** Australia and New Zealand
- ↗ **Size:** Medium
- ⚖ **Weight:** 11–17 lb (5–8 kg)
- ✺ **Color:** Variety of colors
- 🐾 **Character:** Energetic, playful, enthusiastic, and friendly
- 💬 **Voice:** Average purr

Big triangular-shaped ears

All Australian Mists have green eyes.

Extra long whiskers

Short coat is easy to take care of

These cats get their name from the delicate, misty look of their fur.

Korat

This silver-blue stunner is one of the oldest cat breeds. The Korat is considered lucky in Thailand. In the past, a pair of Korats was a popular wedding gift because the breed is said to bring happiness and fortune!

Heart-shaped head with big ears

Big, bright green eyes

Short, dense, coat

Muscular, slim body

Fact file

- 🌍 **Origin:** Thailand
- 🐟 **Size:** Small to medium
- ⚖ **Weight:** 6–10 lb (3–5 kg)
- 🎨 **Color:** Silver-blue
- 🐾 **Character:** Nervous, gentle, affectionate, and alert
- 💬 **Voice:** Quiet

Bombay

This black beauty is sleek and shiny like a miniature panther. But unlike a panther, the Bombay is friendly, fun, and loves cuddling! This breed is closely related to the Burmese.

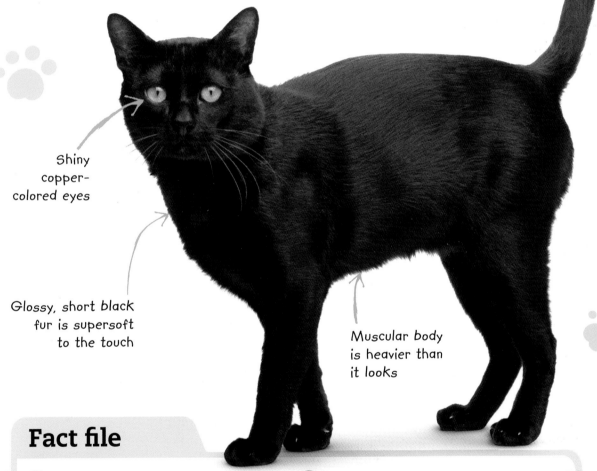

Shiny copper-colored eyes

Glossy, short black fur is supersoft to the touch

Muscular body is heavier than it looks

Fact file

- **Origin:** USA
- **Size:** Medium
- **Weight:** 6–11 lb (2.5–5 kg)
- **Color:** Black
- **Character:** Affectionate, playful, friendly, and intelligent
- **Voice:** Noisy

Singapura

From the island of Singapore comes this tiny fur ball of fun! The world's smallest cat may be tiny but it has a huge personality. Singapuras want plenty of playtime and company.

Big ears sit wide in an alert position

Very big eyes compared to the body size

Small yet stocky and muscular body

Short, fine hairs create bands of brown and cream

Fact file

🌐 **Origin:** Singapore

↗ **Size:** Small to medium

⬤ **Weight:** 4–8 lb (1.5–3.5 kg)

✳ **Color:** Mix of brown and cream

🐾 **Character:** Intelligent, curious, playful, and affectionate

💬 **Voice:** Quiet

Abyssinian

This cat is among the oldest breeds, and looks like the cats from ancient Egyptian paintings and statues. The adventurous Abyssinian is often compared with the African wild cat. They are both eager explorers and skilled hunters.

Gorgeous green eyes are lined with black

Athletic and muscular body shape

Very big, pointed ears

Short, stripy, flecked coat provided camouflage in the wild

Fact file

- **Origin:** Egypt
- **Size:** Medium
- **Weight:** 4–9 lb (2–4 kg)
- **Color:** Variety of colors
- **Character:** Friendly, content, intelligent, and active
- **Voice:** Quiet

Exotics

This type of cat looks and behaves like a longhaired Persian, but the fur is much easier to manage. They come in a lot of colors! Exotics enjoy playtime and cuddling.

Flat face and nose typical of Exotics and Persians

Blue

Gray-brown

Short, strong legs

Short, thick coat is easy to take care of

Fact file

🌐 **Origin:** USA

✖️ **Size:** Medium to large

⚖️ **Weight:** 7–13 lb (3–6 kg)

✳️ **Color:** Various

🐾 **Character:** Sweet, curious, active, and playful

💬 **Voice:** Quiet

Eyes can be various colors depending on the coat color

Cream coat with brown points

Accidental cat
Exotics were created accidentally, when a breeder tried to create a silver American Shorthair.

Large, round head

Small, rounded ears

Blue point

Orange hairs make the fur look golden

An Exotic kitten

Egyptian Mau

Meet the spottiest speed demon! The Mau, meaning "cat" in ancient Egypt, has an eye-catching coat. But the spots blur when the world's fastest domestic cat reaches its top speed of 30 mph (48 kph).

Graceful yet muscular body

Short, silky coat is covered in spots and stripes

Big, green eyes

Fact file

- ⊕ **Origin:** Egypt
- ⤢ **Size:** Medium
- ⬙ **Weight:** 6–13 lb (3–6 kg)
- ❀ **Color:** Silver, bronze, or smoke
- 🐾 **Character:** Playful, loving, loyal, and active
- 💬 **Voice:** Quiet

 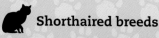

Ocicat

Looks can be deceiving! The Ocicat resembles a wild cat, but the breed is not closely related to the big cats. Instead, it has the lovely looks of a wild cat but all the friendliness of a pet.

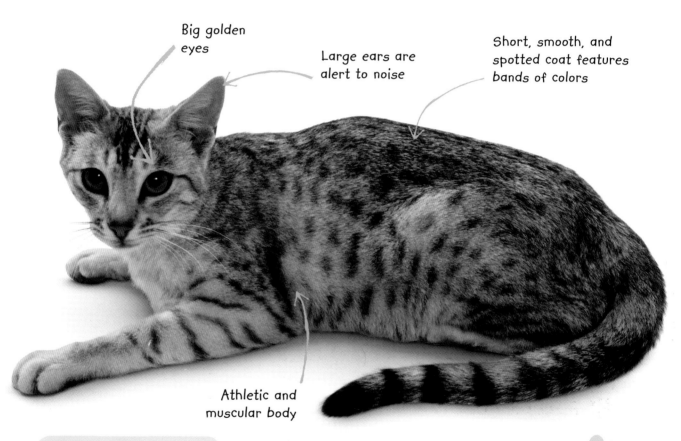

Big golden eyes

Large ears are alert to noise

Short, smooth, and spotted coat features bands of colors

Athletic and muscular body

Fact file

🌐 **Origin:** USA

⚡ **Size:** Medium to large

⚖ **Weight:** 6–15 lb (3–7 kg)

❀ **Color:** Variety of colors

🐾 **Character:** Gentle, loving, curious, and playful

💬 **Voice:** Talkative

Bengal

The Bengal has features like a mini-leopard such as its thick spotted coat, large size, and wild-cat call. But forget jungle hunting, this breed wants backyard games, company, and cuddling!

Long and athletic body lined with muscle

Round-tipped ears with wide bases

Fact file

- 🌐 **Origin:** USA
- ⬚ **Size:** Large
- ⚖ **Weight:** 9–18 lb (4–8 kg)
- ✳ **Color:** Variety of colors
- 🐾 **Character:** Confident, intelligent, active, and affectionate
- 💬 **Voice:** Loud chirrup

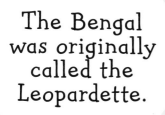

The Bengal was originally called the Leopardette.

Fur is smooth as silk with a shimmering sheen

Exotic **spotted** coat

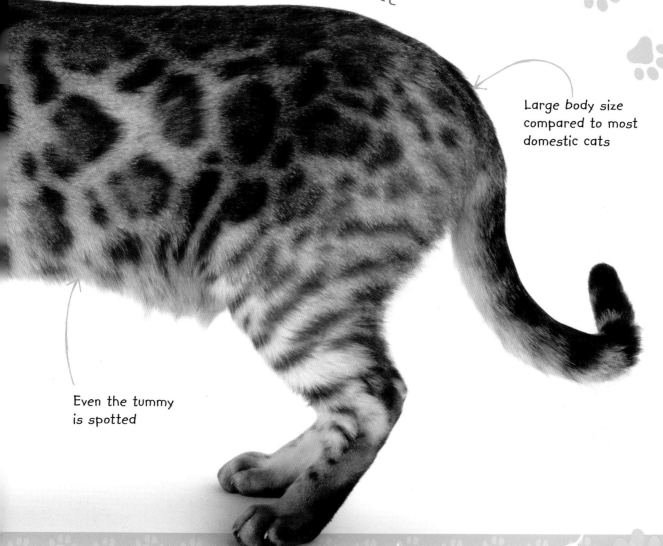

Large body size compared to most domestic cats

Even the tummy is spotted

Chausie

What a whopper! This big boy looks as wild as a jungle cat, but is really a creature of habit. The Chausie sticks to a routine when it comes to sleep and dinnertimes. But the breed also enjoys a lot of play and contact with people.

Big ears

Rough topcoat covering soft undercoat

Large, athletic body

Golden eyes

Long legs

Fact file

🌍 **Origin:** USA

✖ **Size:** Large

⚖ **Weight:** 15–25 lb (7–11 kg)

✳ **Color:** Variety of colors

🐾 **Character:** Relaxed, affectionate, energetic, and playful

💬 **Voice:** Medium

Chartreux

This chunky cutie is a true blue who loves cosy creature comforts and feels happiest at home. French monks first bred the Chartreux hundreds of years ago to keep mice out of monasteries.

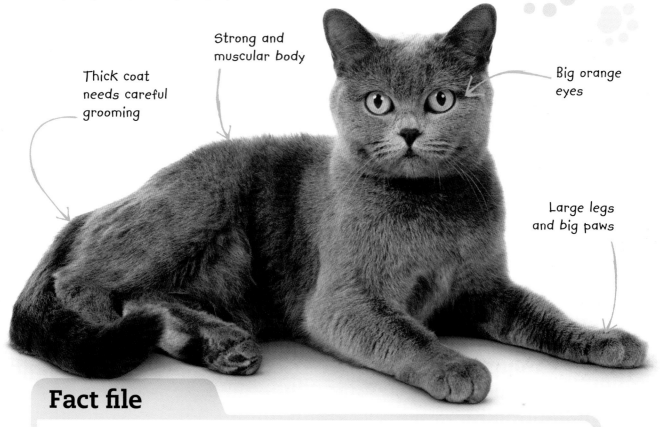

Strong and muscular body

Thick coat needs careful grooming

Big orange eyes

Large legs and big paws

Fact file

- **Origin:** France
- **Size:** Medium to large
- **Weight:** 12–16 lb (5–7 kg)
- **Color:** Blue
- **Character:** Confident, intelligent, affectionate, and gentle
- **Voice:** Quiet

Savannah

The spotted Savannah takes the title of the world's tallest domestic cat. This breed is a cross between a wild African serval and a pet pussycat. It loves exploring, climbing, and jumping.

Giant ears like the serval cat

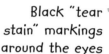

Black "tear stain" markings around the eyes

Big black spots on the fur

Very long legs for a domestic cat

Fact file

- 🌍 **Origin:** USA
- ⤢ **Size:** Large
- ⚖ **Weight:** 12–25 lb (5–11 kg)
- ❀ **Color:** Variety of colors
- 🐾 **Character:** Energetic, intelligent, curious, and friendly
- 💬 **Voice:** Loud hissing sound

Serengeti

Go wild for the Serengeti! This big, beautiful breed is named after an area of Africa that is home to many wild cats. Expect all kinds of action and adventure from this eager explorer.

Long neck held high

Strong and muscular body

Short, smooth, and spotted coat

Big round-tipped ears

Fact file

🧭 **Origin:** USA

↗ **Size:** Medium

⚖ **Weight:** 8–15 lb (4–7 kg)

❋ **Color:** Spotted pattern on golden, gray, or black fur

🐾 **Character:** Friendly, confident, active, and alert

💬 **Voice:** Very talkative

Siamese

This breed came from the royal courts of Siam, now known as Thailand. In addition to their name, Siamese cats have kept their majestic looks and sophisticated manner. They crave company and conversation.

Big pointed ears like a bat

Bright blue eyes

Long and slender legs

Long, elegant body shape

Short, silky coat is mostly cream but dark on the ears, face, paws, and tail

Siamese kittens are born white

Fact file

🌐 **Origin:** Thailand

↗ **Size:** Medium

⬆ **Weight:** 4–11 lb (2–5 kg)

✳ **Color:** Pointed, meaning pale bodies with darker faces, legs, and tails

🐾 **Character:** Intelligent, lively, social, and noisy

💬 **Voice:** Very talkative

Oriental Shorthair

This smart cat is confident, talkative, and enthusiastic about being clean! Brighter than most breeds, the Oriental Shorthair expects a lot of entertainment and play. The Oriental's coat comes in hundreds of colors and patterns.

Large pointed ears

Big eyes can be yellow or green

Long, slim body moves quickly and easily

Longer tail than most breeds

Sleek, short fur is easy to groom

Fact file

- **Origin:** Thailand
- **Size:** Medium
- **Weight:** 8–14lb (3.5–6kg)
- **Color:** Variety of colors
- **Character:** Intelligent, playful, loyal, and affectionate
- **Voice:** Talkative

American Burmese

The Burmese breeds are often called "bricks wrapped in silk." This is because they are much heavier than they look, and their glossy fur is supersoft to the touch. These cats love to hang out with humans.

Muscular and stocky body

Short and silky coat does not need much grooming

Rounder head than the European Burmese

Fact file

⊙ **Origin:** Thailand, Myanmar (formerly Burma)

⤢ **Size:** Medium

⧗ **Weight:** 6–12 lb (3–5 kg)

❋ **Color:** Browns and grays

🐾 **Character:** Affectionate, playful, confident, and friendly

◯ **Voice:** Medium

European Burmese

Brown Burmese cats lived in temples across Asia, many hundreds of years ago. They now have a variety of coat colors. The European Burmese is very similar to the American breed in both looks and personality, but it comes in different colors.

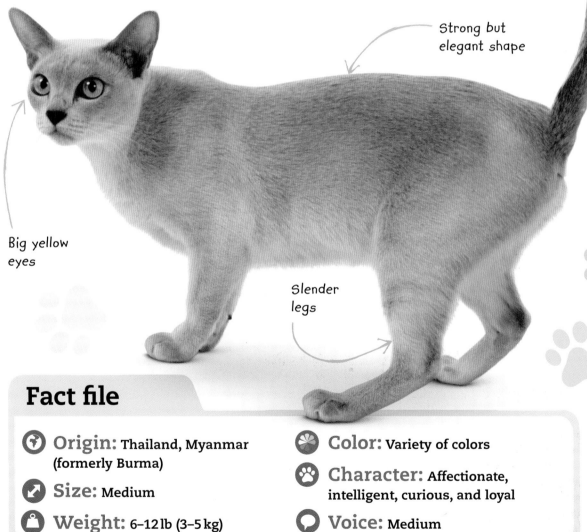

Strong but elegant shape

Big yellow eyes

Slender legs

Fact file

Origin: Thailand, Myanmar (formerly Burma)

Size: Medium

Weight: 6–12 lb (3–5 kg)

Color: Variety of colors

Character: Affectionate, intelligent, curious, and loyal

Voice: Medium

Cornish Rex

The first curly-haired kitten was born in 1950 in Cornwall, UK. Cornish Rexes are known for their covering of curls. The Cornish Rex gets compared to a dog because it enjoys playing fetch, running around, and following family members.

Very big ears sit high on the head

Short, fine coat lies in neat waves

Slim body shape packed with muscles

Fact file

🌐 **Origin:** UK

↗ **Size:** Medium

⚖ **Weight:** 6–9 lb (3–4 kg)

🎨 **Color:** Variety of colors

🐾 **Character:** Intelligent, affectionate, playful, and confident

💬 **Voice:** Talkative

Devon Rex

Another curly-haired kitten was found 10 years after the Cornish Rex, in the nearby county of Devon. The Devon Rex has a pixie face, bat ears, long neck, and of course, a curly coat!

Large ears compared to head size

Even the whiskers are curly

Short curly fur covers the body but it can be very fine in places

Fact file

- 🧭 **Origin:** UK
- 🦴 **Size:** Medium
- ⚖️ **Weight:** 6–9 lb (3–4 kg)
- 🌀 **Color:** Variety of colors
- 🐾 **Character:** Affectionate, energetic, playful, and curious
- 💬 **Voice:** Talkative

Munchkin

This little cat has unusually short, stumpy leg bones. The name "Munchkin" comes from the little people in the children's story *The Wizard of Oz*. Munchkin cats can't jump as well as cats with normal bones.

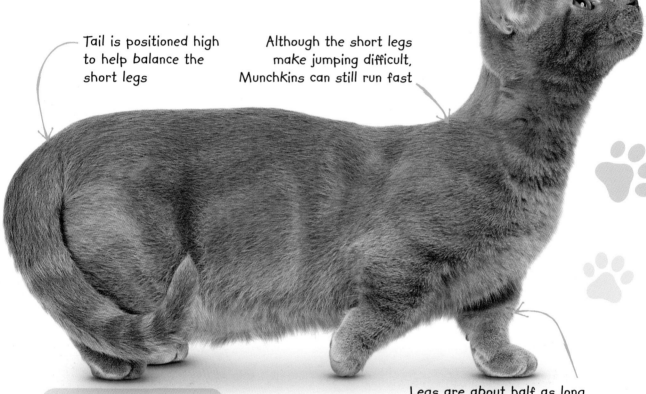

Tail is positioned high to help balance the short legs

Although the short legs make jumping difficult, Munchkins can still run fast

Legs are about half as long as those of other breeds

Fact file

- 🧭 **Origin:** USA
- ↗ **Size:** Small to medium
- ⚖ **Weight:** 5–9 lb (2–4 kg)
- ✳ **Color:** Variety of colors
- 🐾 **Character:** Intelligent, energetic, playful, and affectionate
- 💬 **Voice:** Medium

Sphynx

Like the Munchkin, the Sphynx has unusual genes that mean it doesn't have thick fur to keep it warm. This cat does not like to be fussed over so keep petting and cuddling to a minimum. A weekly bath is important to keep its skin clean.

Skin can be a variety of colors and patterns

Strong and sturdy body shape

Loose skin creates wrinkles on the body

Very short, fine fuzz covers the skin, but cannot be seen

Fact file

- 🌍 **Origin:** Canada
- ↗ **Size:** Medium
- ⚖ **Weight:** 6–11 lb (3–5 kg)
- ❋ **Color:** Variety of colors
- 🐾 **Character:** Energetic, playful, social, and friendly
- 💬 **Voice:** Noisy

Pixiebob

This fabulous feline looks like a wild bobcat but acts like a pet dog. The Pixiebob enjoys playing fetch and other games. Many Pixiebobs like going for walks!

Facial features are similar to a wild bobcat

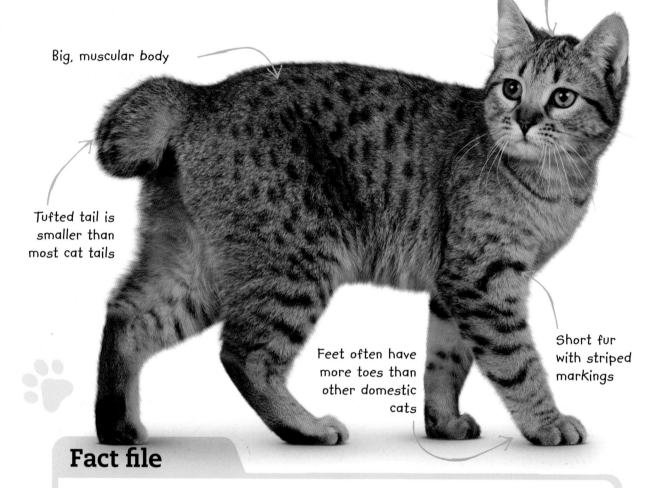

Big, muscular body

Tufted tail is smaller than most cat tails

Feet often have more toes than other domestic cats

Short fur with striped markings

Fact file

- 🌐 **Origin:** USA
- ✖️ **Size:** Medium to large
- ⚖️ **Weight:** 8–17 lb (4–8 kg)
- ❀ **Color:** Brown and black stripes
- 🐾 **Character:** Energetic, social, bold, and intelligent
- 💬 **Voice:** Very vocal

Japanese Bobtail

Don't mistake the Bobtail for a bunny rabbit! This breed has a tiny tail, unlike most other cats. The Japanese bobtail loves talking and cuddling, and is thought to be lucky in Japan.

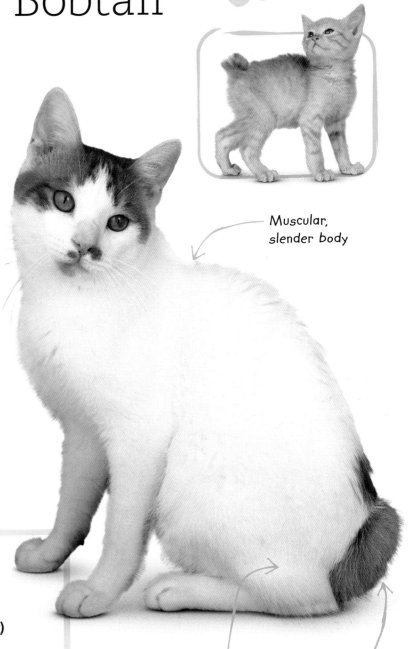

Muscular, slender body

Silky-soft coat comes in different lengths, colors, and patterns

Unusually short tail for a cat

Fact file

- 🌐 **Origin:** Japan
- ◨ **Size:** Medium
- 🏋 **Weight:** 7–11 lb (3–5 kg)
- ◉ **Color:** Variety of colors
- 🐾 **Character:** Reliable, intelligent, playful, and affectionate
- 💬 **Voice:** Range of vocal sounds

Angora

Check out this glamour-puss! The ancient Angora was the first longhaired cat breed in Europe. Whether starring in James Bond movies or stealing the limelight at home, the Angora is always the center of attention.

Shimmering thick fur forms a ruff around the neck

Brushlike tail is longer than average and held upward

Long muscular body

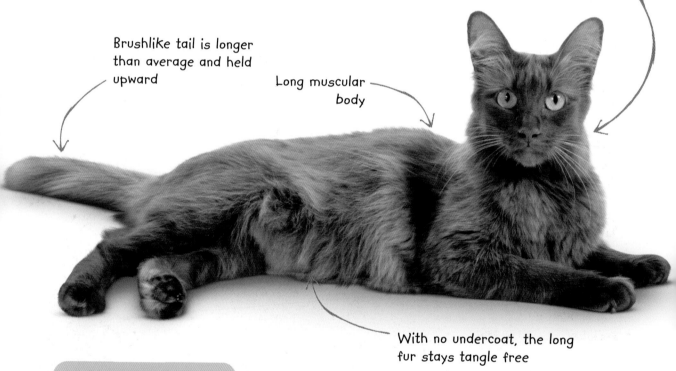

With no undercoat, the long fur stays tangle free

Fact file

- 🌍 **Origin:** Turkey
- ✦ **Size:** Medium
- 🏋 **Weight:** 5–9 lb (2–4 kg)
- ❀ **Color:** Variety of colors
- 🐾 **Character:** Confident, playful, intelligent, and affectionate
- 💬 **Voice:** Loud purr

Persian

Look no further for long, luscious locks! The puffball Persian is one of the oldest breeds. It is instantly recognizable for its flowing fur. Persians like to stay at home getting lots of fuss and attention.

Round, flat face topped by small ears

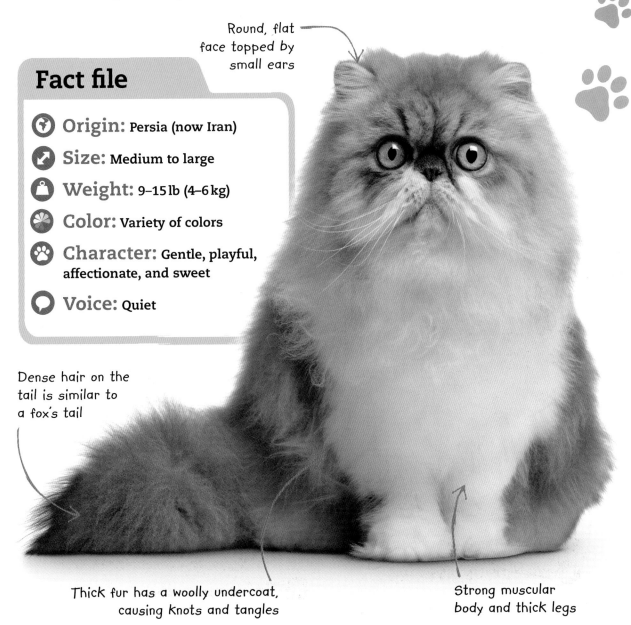

Fact file

- **Origin:** Persia (now Iran)
- **Size:** Medium to large
- **Weight:** 9–15 lb (4–6 kg)
- **Color:** Variety of colors
- **Character:** Gentle, playful, affectionate, and sweet
- **Voice:** Quiet

Dense hair on the tail is similar to a fox's tail

Thick fur has a woolly undercoat, causing knots and tangles

Strong muscular body and thick legs

Ragdoll

Despite being one of the biggest domestic cats, the relaxed Ragdoll is content to just hang out rather then use up a lot of energy. It loves being picked up and cuddled, like a doll.

Beautiful, bright blue eyes

Silky-soft fur

Long and powerful body

Fact file

- ⊕ **Origin:** USA
- ↗ **Size:** Large
- ⚖ **Weight:** 10–20 lb (5–9 kg)
- ✦ **Color:** Variety of colors
- 🐾 **Character:** Calm, gentle, loving, and affectionate
- 💬 **Voice:** Quiet

Maine Coon

The massive Maine Coon came from the US state of Maine. These cool cats are often called "gentle giants" because of their super size and love of playtime and people.

Fluffy ruff around neck

Similar pattern and markings to a raccoon

Enormous bushy tail is at least as long as the body

Long, strong legs

Fact file

- **Origin:** USA
- **Size:** Large
- **Weight:** 11–25 lb (5–11 kg)
- **Color:** Variety of colors
- **Character:** Bold, intelligent, affectionate, and loyal
- **Voice:** Chirping sounds

Himalayan

What do you get if you cross a Persian with a Siamese? A Himalayan! This blue-eyed beauty likes lots of love in quiet surroundings. Be warned though—Himalayans are beautiful but it takes lots of brushing to keep their coats from tangling.

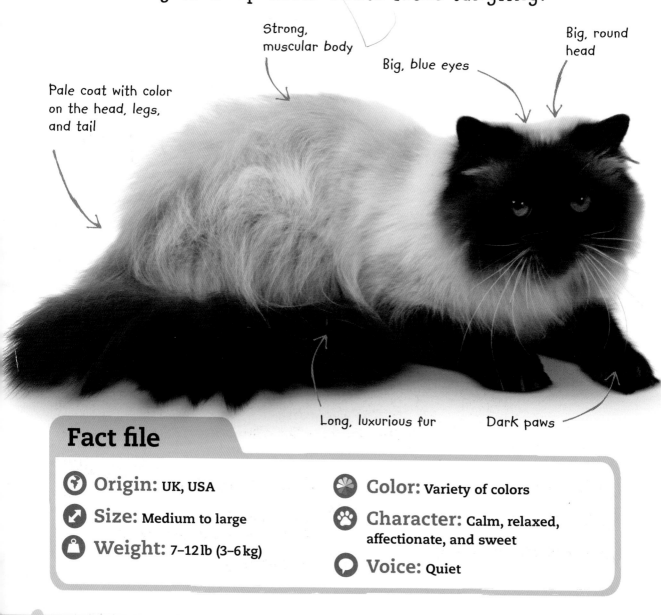

Strong, muscular body

Big, blue eyes

Big, round head

Pale coat with color on the head, legs, and tail

Long, luxurious fur

Dark paws

Fact file

- **Origin:** UK, USA
- **Size:** Medium to large
- **Weight:** 7–12 lb (3–6 kg)
- **Color:** Variety of colors
- **Character:** Calm, relaxed, affectionate, and sweet
- **Voice:** Quiet

LaPerm

Tufted ears

Long, curly whiskers

Stepping out of the hair salon is the LaPerm! Tumbling curls are this cat's trademark, but it is also known for its playful personality. Like curious kittens, LaPerms love to be in the thick of the action.

Muscular body

Coat of loose curls is soft to the touch

Thick tail looks like a brush

Fact file

🧭 **Origin:** USA

↗️ **Size:** Small to medium

⚖️ **Weight:** 5–9 lb (2–4 kg)

🌼 **Color:** Variety of colors

🐾 **Character:** Active, affectionate, social, and playful

💬 **Voice:** Quiet

Birman

The beautiful Birman is called the "sacred cat of Burma." This breed is said to have been created by a blue-eyed goddess, who blessed a temple cat by magically turning its yellow eyes blue.

Bright *blue* eyes

Fact file

🌐 **Origin:** Myanmar (formerly Burma)

⤢ **Size:** Medium

⚖ **Weight:** 6–12 lb (2.5–5 kg)

🎨 **Color:** Pale body with darker patches on the face, legs, and tail

🐾 **Character:** Gentle, relaxed, curious, and intelligent

💬 **Voice:** Soft sounds

Birman kittens are born white and get their dark patches as they grow.

Fur needs **grooming** every day

Birmans have silky coats that are usually cream colored. It does not tangle easily.

Four white paws

Its powerful body is longer than most long-haired cats.

Norwegian Forest Cat

Fairy tales in Scandinavian countries often feature this fluffiest of felines. The Norwegian forest cat is a skilled climber, with a fur coat fully equipped for the coldest winters.

Fact file

- **Origin:** Norway
- **Size:** Large
- **Weight:** 9–20 lb (4–9 kg)
- **Color:** Variety of colors
- **Character:** Intelligent, social, alert, and gentle
- **Voice:** Quiet

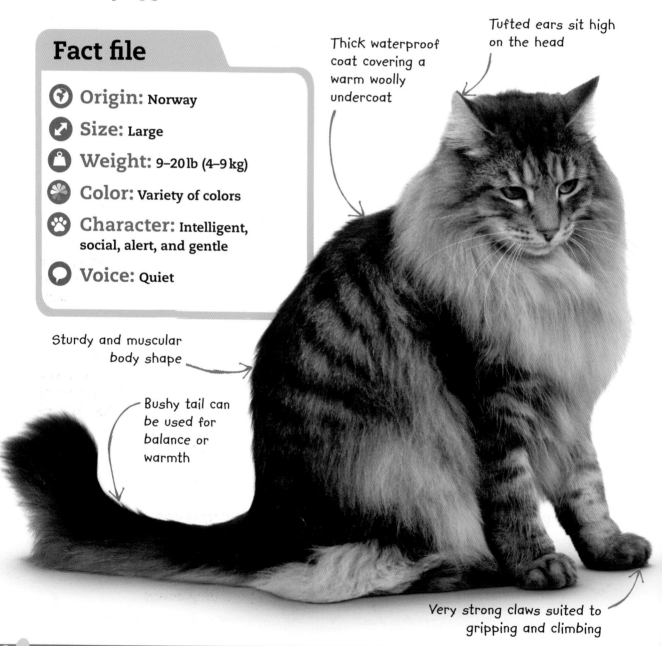

Thick waterproof coat covering a warm woolly undercoat

Tufted ears sit high on the head

Sturdy and muscular body shape

Bushy tail can be used for balance or warmth

Very strong claws suited to gripping and climbing

Siberian Forest Cat

This superfurry cat has a very thick coat. This kept it warm in its original home in the frozen forests of Siberia.

Round eyes are usually green or gold

Long and bushy tail provides balance when jumping

Strong and muscular body

Longer back legs help with jumping and climbing

Three-layered coat needs regular brushing to avoid tangles and hair balls

Large, round paws balance the big body weight

Fact file

🌐 **Origin:** Siberia, Russia

↗ **Size:** Medium to large

⚖ **Weight:** 8–20 lb g (3.5–9 k)

🎨 **Color:** Variety of colors

🐾 **Character:** Affectionate, athletic, active, and playful

💬 **Voice:** Chirping noises

Somali

Look up high for a Somali cat! They love climbing trees or hanging out near the ceiling. These curious cats always have their eyes on the next adventure. The earliest Somali cats were superfurry versions of the Abyssinian breed.

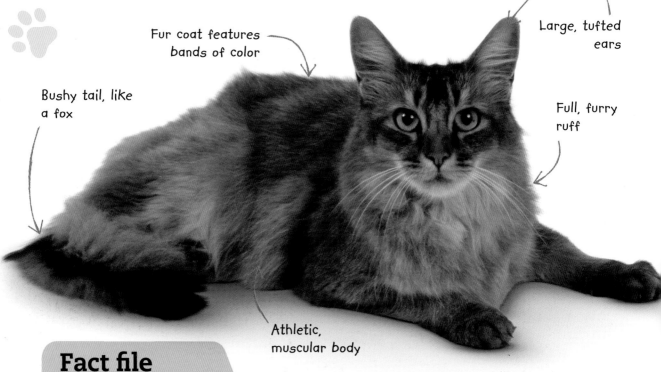

Fur coat features bands of color

Large, tufted ears

Bushy tail, like a fox

Full, furry ruff

Athletic, muscular body

Fact file

- 🌍 **Origin:** USA, Australia
- ↗ **Size:** Medium
- ⚖ **Weight:** 6–12 lb (2.5–5.5 kg)
- ❁ **Color:** Variety of colors
- 🐾 **Character:** Gentle, playful, intelligent, and lively
- 💬 **Voice:** Quiet

Balinese

Known for their elegance, these cats were named after graceful dancers from the Asian island of Bali. Balinese cats are the same as Siamese cats, but with long hair.

Bright-blue eyes

Slender body shape

Small, dainty paws

Long, silky fur coat

Fact file

- **Origin:** USA
- **Size:** Medium
- **Weight:** 4–11 lb (2–5 kg)
- **Character:** Loving, curious, active, and social
- **Color:** Pointed, meaning pale bodies with darker faces, legs, and tails
- **Voice:** Talkative

Turkish Van

This breed comes from Turkey, where it is thought to be lucky. Also called the "swimming cat," the Turkish Van enjoys the water.

Eyes are mostly gold or blue, but can be different colors

Strong, athletic body for speedy movement in water

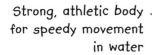

Pink nose turns red if the Turkish Van is upset

Coat of silky white fur is easy to comb

Fact file

🌐 **Origin:** Turkey

↗ **Size:** Medium to large

⚖ **Weight:** 10–18 lb (4–8 kg)

❂ **Color:** White body with a colored head and tail

🐾 **Character:** Active, intelligent, playful, and independent

💬 **Voice:** Very vocal with lots of meows and mews

Turkish Angora

Blue or green eyes

This ancient breed is considered a national treasure in Turkey. The Turkish Angora is a water baby who loves life on the go. Climbing, playing tricks, and dipping its paws in water are favorite activities!

Silky, soft coat

Graceful yet strong body

Fact file

- **Origin:** Turkey
- **Size:** Medium
- **Weight:** 5–12 lb (2–5.5 kg)
- **Color:** Usually white but can be a variety of colors
- **Character:** Lively, affectionate, energetic, and demanding
- **Voice:** Talkative

Nebelung

This rare breed's name is German for "creature of the mist." The Nebelung loves keeping the same company and routine, so avoid introducing strangers or making changes to its home life.

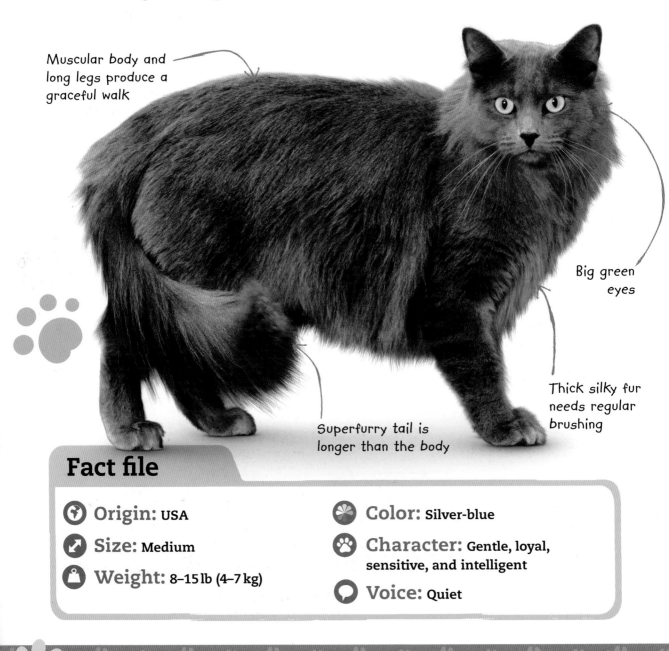

Muscular body and long legs produce a graceful walk

Big green eyes

Thick silky fur needs regular brushing

Superfurry tail is longer than the body

Fact file

- **Origin:** USA
- **Size:** Medium
- **Weight:** 8–15 lb (4–7 kg)
- **Color:** Silver-blue
- **Character:** Gentle, loyal, sensitive, and intelligent
- **Voice:** Quiet

Selkirk Rex

This curly cat is a big softie! The sweet-natured Selkirk wants lots of love. With fur this silky soft, it is sure to get snuggles galore. The special curled coat has given the breed a nickname "the cat in sheep's clothing."

The Selkirk can be either longhaired or shorthaired.

Fact file

- 🌐 **Origin:** USA
- ⬈ **Size:** Medium to large
- 🏋 **Weight:** 10–15 lb (4.5–7 kg)
- ✿ **Color:** Variety of colors
- 🐾 **Character:** Loving, social, patient, and relaxed
- 💬 **Voice:** Quiet

Rounded head with very full cheeks

Thick curly coat needs careful grooming

Big, muscular body

Neck, tummy, and tail are the curliest

Tiffanie

Look no further for cat communication!
Whether chatting away to its owner or
protesting at being left alone, this
longhaired member of the Asian cat
family always makes its voice heard.

Green or
yellow eyes

Firm body is heavier
than it looks

Silky, fine hair does
not get tangled

Flowing, furry tail

Fact file

🌐 **Origin:** UK

↗ **Size:** Medium

⚖ **Weight:** 9–15 lb (4–7 kg)

❀ **Color:** Variety of colors

🐾 **Character:** Affectionate,
playful, intelligent, and demanding

💬 **Voice:** Vocal

Chantilly

Cats don't come much cuter than the Chantilly. Checking all the boxes for silky, soft, and sweet, this breed loves responding to conversation with chirping sounds. Some say this intelligent cat can even sing!

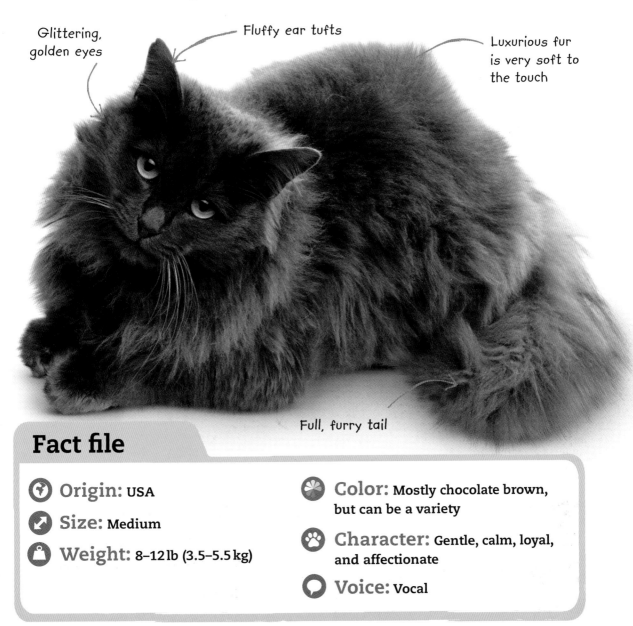

Glittering, golden eyes

Fluffy ear tufts

Luxurious fur is very soft to the touch

Full, furry tail

Fact file

- **Origin:** USA
- **Size:** Medium
- **Weight:** 8–12 lb (3.5–5.5 kg)
- **Color:** Mostly chocolate brown, but can be a variety
- **Character:** Gentle, calm, loyal, and affectionate
- **Voice:** Vocal

Scottish Fold

The first thing to notice about this Scottish sweetheart is its neatly folded ears. The Scottish Fold was discovered by a shepherd who spotted an unusual kitten with folded ears in 1961.

Round head with chunky cheeks

Each ear bends downward with a clear fold

Big, bright eyes

The Scottish Fold's thick fur can be short or long.

Scottish Fold kittens' ears start to fold down after a few weeks.

Long, bushy tail

Fact file

- 🌐 **Origin:** Scotland, UK
- ↗ **Size:** Medium
- ⚖ **Weight:** 6–13 lb (2.5–6 kg)
- 🎨 **Color:** Variety of colors
- 🐾 **Character:** Loving, relaxed, intelligent, and affectionate
- 💬 **Voice:** Quiet

Manx

The marvelous Manx is the subject of many legends, but its missing tail is a genetic defect rather than anything magical. Most cats use their tails for balance, but the Manx breed is thought to have extrasensitive inner ears to help its balancing act.

Strong and sturdy body

Short, dense coat

Fact file

- 🌍 **Origin:** Isle of Man
- ✥ **Size:** Medium
- ⚖ **Weight:** 8–12 lb (3.5–5.5 kg)
- ✹ **Color:** Variety of colors
- 🐾 **Character:** Intelligent, playful, affectionate, and alert
- 💬 **Voice:** Quiet

Good **hunters**

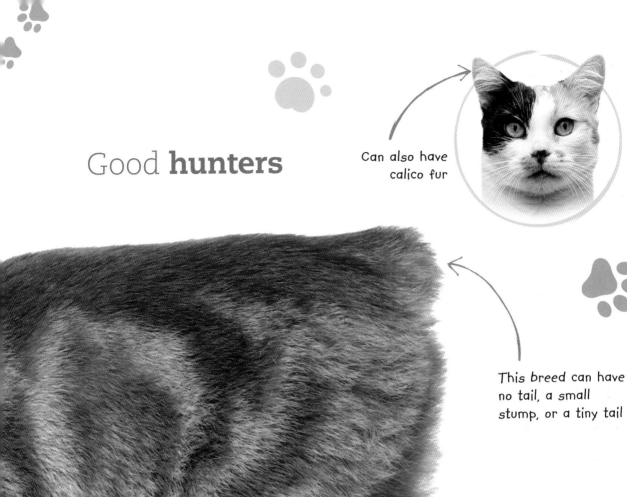

Can also have calico fur

This breed can have no tail, a small stump, or a tiny tail

Longer back legs are rabbitlike

Some Manx cats can be trained to play "fetch."

House cats

House cats are cats of no particular breed. Millions of them are kept as pets around the world, making them the most common domestic cat. House cats can be big or small, have long or short hair, and be patterned or plain.

House-cat fur can be any color or pattern

Fur type varies for house cats

Strong and robust body with few health problems

Fact file

- 🌐 **Origin:** Britain
- ↗ **Size:** Varied
- ⚖ **Weight:** 5–12 lb (2.5–5.5 kg)
- ✿ **Color:** Variety of colors
- 🐾 **Character:** Independent, affectionate, playful, and content
- 💬 **Voice:** Medium

Eyes can be a range of colors

Many house cats
There are over 500 million domestic cats in the world and they're mostly just house cats!

Most house cats have short fur that is easy to take care of

Most cats have an average of four kittens per litter

House cats make great pets and are known for being wonderful companions.

Quiz—test your cat knowledge!

Cats come in so many shapes and sizes, and they are found on every continent except Antarctica. How much do you know about the amazing world of cats and kittens?

1. Which of these cats is famous for swimming?
- ☐ **a)** Persian
- ☐ **b)** Turkish Van
- ☐ **c)** Munchkin

2. How high can cats jump?
- ☐ **a)** Half their own height.
- ☐ **b)** Three times their own height.
- ☐ **c)** Seven times their own height.

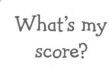

What's my score?

3. Which of these sounds means you should leave your cat alone?
- ☐ **a)** Growl
- ☐ **b)** Chirp
- ☐ **c)** Purr

4. Which of these should you NOT give your cat?

☐ **a)** A bowl of fresh water
☐ **b)** A bowl of dry food
☐ **c)** A bar of chocolate

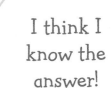

I think I know the answer!

5. Which of these is the biggest cat in the world?

☐ **a)** Maine Coon
☐ **b)** Singapura
☐ **c)** Abyssinian

6. How many hours a day can a cat sleep?

☐ **a)** 6 hours a day.
☐ **b)** 18 hours a day
☐ **c)** 24 hours a day

7. At what age do cats start to walk?

☐ **a)** Three days
☐ **b)** Three weeks
☐ **c)** Three years

Answers:

1.b) 2.c) 3.a) 4.c) 5.a) 6.b) 7.b)

Glossary

Affectionate Warm and loving.

Allergy Bad reaction to something, which gives a person or cat watery eyes and makes them sneeze.

Ancient Very old.

Big cat Large, wild members of the cat family, such as lions.

Breed Type of cat with specific characteristics.

Breeder Person who arranges for kittens to be born with certain looks and personalities.

Camouflage Color or markings of an animal that help it blend in with the surroundings.

Carnivore Animal with biting teeth that eats a diet of meat.

Catnip Plant that produces a scented oil that cats love.

Dandruff Flakes of skin.

Claws Sharp nails at the end of a paw or foot.

Domestic Animal that is taken care of by people.

Feline A cat or something that is catlike.

Flexible Something that bends without breaking.

Fur Soft hair that grows over most of a cat's body to keep it warm.

Genes Pieces of information inherited from parents.

Grooming Taking care of fur or hair so it stays clean and neat.

Instinct Natural desire to do something.

Keratin Substance found in hair, claws, and fingernails.

Kitten Young cat.

Litter Group of baby kittens born to the same mother at the same time.

Litter box Plastic box that cats use as their toilet.

Longhair Cat with long, thick hair.

Pedigree Animal whose parents are both of the same breed.

Prey Animal that is killed by another animal.

Protein Substance found in foods such as meat and eggs.

Pupil Dark center of the eye.

Queen Pregnant cat.

Senses Animal's view of the world through the five senses of sight, smell, hearing, taste, and touch.

Serval Wild cat that lives on African grasslands and savannas, with spotted fur and long legs.

Shorthair Cat with short hair or fur.

Sibling Brother or sister.

Spontaneous Do something suddenly.

Tame Used to having contact with people.

Therapy Treatment designed to help with people's health and happiness.

Weaning Process in which very young kittens stop drinking their mother's milk.

Whiskers Stiff, sensitive hairs sprouting from a cat's face.

Wild Animal living free in the outside world.

Index

Acknowledgments

DK would like to thank:

Shalini Agrawal and Shambhavi Thatte for editorial work; Amina Youssef and Elise Middleton for additional editorial; Nidhi Mehra and Jaileen Kaur for design work; Kitty Glavin and Eleanor Bates for additional design; Dheeraj Singh for CTS; Rajesh Singh and Vijay Kandwal for hi-res image work; Rituraj Singh and Surya Sarangi for picture research; and Helen Peters for preparing the index.

The publisher would like to thank the following for their kind permission to reproduce their photographs:

(Key: a-above; b-below/bottom; c-center; f-far; l-left; r-right; t-top)

2 123RF.com: andreykuzmin (b). 3 Dreamstime.com: Isselee (b). 4 123RF.com: Anan Kaewkhammul / anankkml (br). Dreamstime.com: Karin Van Ijzendoorn / Satara910 (cla). iStockphoto.com: Vectorig (clb). 5 Animal Photography: Helmi Flick (cr). Dreamstime.com: Dreamzdesigner (clb/map illustration). 6 Alamy Stock Photo: petographer (bc). 7 iStockphoto.com: Vectorig (tl). 8-9 Alamy Stock Photo: Juniors Bildarchiv GmbH (c). 9 iStockphoto.com: ahloch (clb); vvvita (cr); magdasmith (tr). 10 Animal Photography: Helmi Flick (crb). 11 Animal Photography: Tetsu Yamazaki (crb). 14-15 iStockphoto.com: cynoclub (b). 17 123RF.com: Alta Oosthuizen (tl). 18-19 123RF.com: Yuliia Sonsedska (c). 20 123RF.com: Melissa Toledo (cra); Александр Ермолаев (cl, bc). 21 123RF.com: andreykuzmin (bl); Sergey Taran (c); Александр Ермолаев (cr); Maciej Maksymowicz (br); Inna Astakhova (c). 22 iStockphoto.com: Silvia Jansen (bl). 23 123RF.com: Eric Isselee (cla). 24 Dreamstime.com: Mimnr1 (cl). 25 123RF.com: Александр Ермолаев (cla). Dorling Kindersley: Tracy Morgan Animal Photography/ Pat Cherry (cr). 26 123RF.com: Miroslav Beneda (crb); David Carillet (clb). iStockphoto.com: Vectorig (cla, ca, cra). 27 Alamy Stock Photo: Tierfotoagentur (cl). iStockphoto.com: Vectorig (ca, cra). 28 123RF.com: Olga Sapegina (b). 29 123RF.com: bloodua (cr). iStockphoto.com: Mordolff (tr). 32-33 123RF.com: Vladimir Cosic (b). 32 iStockphoto.com: AkilinaWinner (c). 33 123RF.com: budabar (tl). 34 iStockphoto.com: vertraut (bl). 35 123RF.com: Elnur Amikishiyev (cr). Dreamstime.com: Kruglik (clb). 36 iStockphoto.com: totophotos (clb). 37 123RF.com: Maxim Blinkov (cl); Александр Ермолаев (br). 38 Animal Photography: Tetsu Yamazaki (c). 39 123RF.com: Christos Georghiou (br). Fotolia: Olga Drabovich (c). iStockphoto.com: Vectorig (bc). 40-41 Animal Photography: Helmi Flick (c). 40 Animal Photography: Helmi Flick (cla). 41 123RF.com: Christos Georghiou (br). iStockphoto.com: Vectorig (bc). 43 123RF.com: Christos Georghiou (br). iStockphoto.com: Vectorig (bc). 45 123RF.com: Christos Georghiou (br). iStockphoto.com: Vectorig (bc). 47 123RF.com: Christos Georghiou (br); somchai siriwanarangson (bc). iStockphoto.com: Vectorig (bc/Cat Silhouette). 49 123RF.com: Christos Georghiou (br). iStockphoto.com:

Vectorig (bc). 51 123RF.com: Christos Georghiou (br). iStockphoto.com: Vectorig (bc). 52 Animal Photography: Helmi Flick (c). 53 123RF.com: Christos Georghiou (br). iStockphoto.com: Vectorig (bc). 54 Animal Photography: Tetsu Yamazaki (c). 55 123RF.com: Christos Georghiou (br). iStockphoto.com: KrissiLundgren (clb); Vectorig (bc). SuperStock: Juniors (cr). 57 123RF.com: Christos Georghiou (br). iStockphoto.com: Vectorig (bc). 58 123RF.com: Dmitry Kalinovsky (c). 59 123RF.com: Christos Georghiou (br). iStockphoto.com: Vectorig (bc). 60 Dreamstime.com: Oleg Kozlov (clb). 61 123RF.com: Christos Georghiou (br). iStockphoto.com: Vectorig (bc). 62 Dreamstime.com: Ekaterina Cherkashina (c). 63 123RF.com: Christos Georghiou (br). Dorling Kindersley: Tracy Morgan Animal Photography / Susan Ketcher (r, cl). iStockphoto.com: Vectorig (bc). 64 Chanan Photography: (c). 65 123RF.com: Christos Georghiou (br). Alamy Stock Photo: Juniors Bildarchiv GmbH (tr). Animal Photography: Alan Robinson (cr). iStockphoto.com: Vectorig (bc). 67 123RF.com: Christos Georghiou (br). Dreamstime.com: Isselee (cb). iStockphoto.com: Vectorig (bc). 69 123RF.com: Christos Georghiou (br). iStockphoto.com: Vectorig (bc). 71 123RF.com: Christos Georghiou (br). Animal Photography: Helmi Flick (c). iStockphoto.com: Vectorig (bc). 73 123RF.com: Christos Georghiou (br). iStockphoto.com: GlobalP (tl); Vectorig (bc). 75 123RF.com: Christos Georghiou (br). Animal Photography: Tetsu Yamazaki (c). iStockphoto.com: Vectorig (bc). 76 Dreamstime.com: Nataliya Kuznetsova / Dobermanstudio (cra). 77 123RF.com: Christos Georghiou (br). iStockphoto.com: Vectorig (bc). 78 Ardea: Jean-Michel Labat (c). 79 123RF.com: Christos Georghiou (br). iStockphoto.com: Vectorig (bc). 80 Animal Photography: Tetsu Yamazaki (c). 81 123RF.com: Christos Georghiou (br). Animal Photography: Tetsu Yamazaki (crb). iStockphoto.com: Vectorig (bc). 83 123RF.com: Christos Georghiou (br). iStockphoto.com: Vectorig (bc). 84 Dorling Kindersley: Tracy Morgan Animal Photography / Jan Bradley (clb). 85 123RF.com: Christos Georghiou (br). iStockphoto.com: Vectorig (bc). 87 123RF.com: Christos Georghiou (br). iStockphoto.com: Vectorig (bc). 89 123RF.com: Christos Georghiou (br). iStockphoto.com: Vectorig (bc). 90 Ardea: Jean-Michel Labat (cl). 93 Animal Photography: Tetsu Yamazaki (bl). 96 123RF.com: Maciej Maksymowicz (b).

Cover images: Front: Fotolia: Roman Milert br; Getty Images: StockImage bl; Warren Photographic Limited: cla; Back: 123RF.com: Oksana Kuzmina tr; Dreamstime.com: Vladyslav Starozhylov cb; Warren Photographic Limited: ca; Spine: iStockphoto.com: KrissiLundgren cb.

All other images © Dorling Kindersley
For further information see: www.dkimages.com